The Secret of Imagining

NEVILLE GODDARD

GENERAL PRESS

Published by
GENERAL PRESS
4805/24, Fourth Floor, Krishna House
Ansari Road, Daryaganj, New Delhi - 110002
Ph : 011-23282971, 45795759
E-mail : generalpressindia@gmail.com

www.generalpress.in

First Edition : 2021

ISBN : 9789354991271

Published by Azeem Ahmad Khan for General Press

BESTSELLING NON-FICTION

- Relativity by Albert Einstein
  Science/Physics, ISBN: 9789380914220
- Reminiscences of a Stock Operator by Edwin Lefevre
  Business/Stock Market, ISBN: 9788194764816
- Success Through a Positive Mental Attitude by Napoleon Hill
  Self-Help, ISBN: 9789390492435
- The Art of War by Sun Tzu
  Self-Help, ISBN: 9789380914893
- The Autobiography of a Yogi by Paramahansa Yogananda
  Biographies & Memoirs, ISBN: 9789380914602
- The Diary of a Young Girl by Anne Frank
  Biographies & Memoirs, ISBN: 9789380914312
- The Elements of Style by William Strunk
  Non-Fiction, ISBN: 9789389157123
- The Law of Success by Napoleon Hill
  Self-Help, ISBN: 9788180320927
- The Power of Your Subconscious Mind by Joseph Murphy
  Self-Help, ISBN: 9788180320958
- The Richest Man in Babylon by George S. Clason
  Business & Economics, ISBN: 9789387669369
- The Science of Getting Rich by Wallace D. Wattles
  Self-Help, ISBN: 9788180320972
- The World as I See It by Albert Einstein
  Non-Fiction, ISBN: 9789388118125

Search the book by its ISBN

About the Author

Neville Goddard was an articulate and charismatic individual who preached a philosophy termed 'New Thought'. Born in St. Michael, Barbados in 1905, Neville was a middle child in a large family of nine boys and one girl. He journeyed over to the United States in 1922 to study drama at seventeen years of age. During this time, he became a dancer, married his first wife, and had a son named Joseph Neville Goddard.

While touring in England with his dance company, he became entwined with the enigma of metaphysics after receiving books from a noble gentleman on the subject. After returning to New York, he dismissed his desire for the entertainment world and committed himself to the learning of spiritual matters until his death in 1972. Carried by a self-taught enthusiasm of the workings of metaphysics, Neville encapsulated the translucency of creative thinking like no other New Though figure of his time.

After the breakdown of his first marriage, Neville was single for a number of years until the 1930s when he met his second wife, a designer, and had a daughter named Victoria.

Neville was drafted into the United States Army at the age of 38 in 1943. This made him uneasy seeing that he felt he was too old, in addition to having a wife and child dependent on him. Neville put his teaching to use and through the power of 'seeing himself out of the army', Neville was honorably discharged after only a few weeks in training. However, one good thing came out of it for him, he received his US citizenship.

Even though Neville could quote from the Bible with vivid aplomb, he seemed tense when trying to compress it all into a psychological concept. In his eye, the Bible was an allegorical tale, and that each character portrayed was a symbol, a lesson, a thought, a point of wisdom.

Most people that are familiar with Neville Goddards work are likely to quote either from the Law or The Promise, but there was a third aspect to his teaching and that was of revision. This concept allowed you to rewrite as it were, any bad or misdirected event in your life and revise it to create a new outcome.

In every life, a little rain must fall and Neville Goddard certainly had his share. An individual by the name of Israel Regardie thought deeply of the escalating New Though movement. He focused intensely on Neville, whose philosophy, he believed, mirrored both the limitations and hopes of the New Thought values. He stated "Neville's metaphysical methods are exquisite; nonetheless, it requires a discipline, an approach that allows individuals to enter the portals of metaphysics. Without this training, his method may work for him, but how about others who do not have this mental discipline?"

Neville never had the success of Ernest Holmes or Norman Vincent Peale. Yet, at the pinnacle of his career, he had thousands of believers. In San Francisco, Los Angeles, and New York, he lectured to crowds in packed auditoriums and churches. He succeeded in having a radio program, and for a while, an inspiring TV show transmitted from Los Angeles during the mid 1950s. His teachings were spread through books and lectures, and he generously permitted students to tape his lectures minus any cost.

During the last twelve-years of his life, Neville's philosophy took an extreme turn, a turn that would be a disadvantage to his popularity in metaphysics. He spoke of a grating supernatural experience that took place in 1959. Neville said he was "renewed as a child from inside his skull, which opened like a womb." In a difficult elucidation of the Bible and his own experience, he spoke of 'the promise', that all of us are waiting to be freed through metaphysical fulfillment. Our imaginations, factually, is the God beginning. He related to Psalm 82:6 as the actual truth of man's state.

Throughout his lectures, Neville Goddard moved his focus to the mystical story of rebirth. This made his audience uneasy, since they preferred the clear, positive, metaphysical approach. Though when he passed away, supposedly of a brain aneurysm in 1972, an obituary was nowhere to be found, even in Los Angeles, a place he considered his home. Whatever his curse or kismet, or maybe because of them, Neville Goddard was one of the most incredible metaphysical teachers in the last century.

Neville Goddard Wrote 10 books in his career included below:

At Your Command

Awakened Imagination & The Search

Feeling is the Secret

Freedom For All

Out of This World

Prayer, The Art of Believing

Seedtime and Harvest

The Law and The Promise

The Power of Awareness

Your Faith is Your Fortune

THE SECRET OF IMAGINING

In almost every particular is the world about us different from what we think it. Why then should we be so incredulous? Life calls on us to believe not less, but more. The secret of imaging is the greatest of all problems, to the solution of which everyone should aspire, for supreme power, supreme wisdom, supreme delight lie in the solution of this mystery.

If you have solved the mystery of imagining you have found Jesus Christ. Jesus Christ is defined for us in scripture as "The power of God and the wisdom of God" (First Corinthians 1:24). As we are told in the eighth chapter of the Book of Proverbs,—and Wisdom is speaking now, personified as a little child:

> *"When He laid out the foundation of the world*
> *I was beside Him like a little child*
> *I was daily His delight,*
> *rejoicing before Him always*
> *rejoicing in His inhabited world,*
> *delighting in the affairs of men.*
> *He who finds me finds life*
> *He who misses me injures himself;*
> *All who hate me love death."*

—Proverbs 8:29-31, 35, 36

So find that child that is the symbol of Jesus Christ, who is the creative power and the wisdom of God. Believe me when I tell you that this Jesus Christ of scripture is your own wonderful human imagination. "By him all things were made, and without him was not anything made that was made" (John 1:3). He is in the world, and the world was made by Him, and the world knows Him not.

Look into the world and name one thing that wasn't first imagined. You name one thing that does not now exist in your imagination—just name it. Name anything in the world that does not now exist in your imagination: "All things exist in the human imagination." (from "Jerusalem" by William Blake)

"God is man, and exists in us and we in Him" (from "Annotations to Berkeley" by William Blake). The eternal abode of man is the imagination; and that is God Himself. Try to disprove it.

God is my pure imagining in myself. He underlies all of my faculties, including perception, but He streams into my surface mind least disguised in the form of productive fancy. I can catch Him in the act of producing these images in my mind. Just try it as you are seated here. Try to think of anything. Try to catch Him in the act of actually producing in your own mind's eye all these images. "For all things exist in the human imagination." But how can I single out one and clothe it so that it becomes an objective fact?

That is the secret, for they all exist within me. But how can I catch one and clothe it? Well I will try to show you tonight what I know from my own personal experience. Scripture teaches it, but it tells it in a strange and wonderful way: how to clothe it.

You see this room in which we are now? It's more real now than your own home is to you; yet you know your home more intimately than you know this room. Yet this room, at the moment, while you are in it, is more real than your own home. How different the cubic reality from the plane of any depiction of it. This room is now so "real" because we are in it, and we are all imagination. We're in it; and to us, it's real. Think of your own home. Do we not have the capacity to draw it, to paint it? But in your mind's eye you have a plane depiction of it, but it's not as real now as the room is. This room is real because we're in it.

Now this is what I mean by making something that is only a thought—something that is real. How do I do it? I single out, out of my own wonderful human imagination, that which I want to make real. It's all in you. Then I must enter into it as I have entered into this room. "If the spectator would enter into any one of these images in his imagination, approaching it on the fiery chariot of his own contemplative thought" (from "Visions of the Last Judgment" by William Blake), it would become just as real to him as this room.

You may ask, "What would that do to me? Will it become real in the not-distant future?" I know from my own experience, it will. You can sit here and enter into a state. It may not take on quite the reality of this room, but it will if you persist in it; it will become just like this. When you open your eyes, it vanishes. But does it mean that I tasted that, and that's all? No. Having gone into it, may I tell you, it will follow you? It will not recede into the past as memory; it will advance into the future and you will confront it. This is the secret of imaging, which is finding out the secret of God.

You are an immortal being. You cannot die because you are all imagination. Man is all imagination; and God truly is man; and He exists in us, and we in Him. And that immortal body of man is the human imagination, and that is Jesus Christ Himself,—the Eternal Body of man and it cannot die. You cannot die. The body,—yes, this will fade; but I am not the garment that I am wearing. I am the wearer of the garment, and the wearer of this garment is all imagination. This is the story that the Bible teaches.

When we read in the Bible: "I, even I, am He. I kill, and I make alive; I wound, and I heal; and there is no god beside me" (Deuteronomy 32:39). This is not a being outside of you speaking; this is the Being that you really are, speaking within you, trying to persuade Himself of His own wonderful power to create. It can kill, and yet it can make alive. It can resurrect from the dead. And that is your own wonderful human imagination.

The day will come; you will taste this power that you possess. You will come into a room just like this, and you will still it—not by commanding anyone in the room to be still. Leave them just as they are. But you will arrest within yourself an activity that you feel, and as you still it in you, everything that you observe becomes still—perfectly still. You could go forward and examine them, and they are dead. Everything is perfectly still and dead. The life is in you. You release the activity, and they once more become animated and continue to do what they intended to do. You could, when you stilled the activity within you, change their motivation; and when you release it, they will do entirely different from what they intended to do prior to your arrestment within you of that activity.

"As the Father has life in Himself, He has granted the Son also to have life in Himself" (John 5:26); and you have that within you. You're not quite aware of it yet, but you will become aware. Those that I am teaching will have dreams, as you have dreams; and in their dreams they will become awake, and then arrest it in the dream and change the motivation and see the intended act change.

Here is one. A friend became aware that she was dreaming, and here's a man who intended to hurt her. He got out of the car and came towards her, and she became afraid; and her fright woke her; but instead of walking on the bed, she awoke in the dream. Then she realized, "This is what he teaches. Now I will simply arrest it." She didn't argue with him; she arrested, within her, the activity that animated him. And she said to him, "You are tired. You need a good hot cup of coffee and then a good sound sleep," and then she told him exactly what he needed, and released the activity within her. He shook his head as though something strange had happened within him, and he got back into the car—all in her dream—and drove off. You see, she changed his intention towards her.

This may seem impossible to the world. As I started this lecture, almost everything in this world is so completely unlike what it appears to be. And I am telling you from my own experience; I am not speculating. I am not theorizing. The power of which I speak is a power within you. That power is not something on the outside; it's your own wonderful human imagination, and you will learn to control it. Your imagination animates the world in which you live. You change your imagination, and you change the world.

To attempt to change circumstances before I change my own imaginal activity is to struggle against the very nature of my own being, for my own imaginal activity is animating my world. If I believe that I am injured or that others are against me, I have conjured them in my world, and they have to be against me. If I fully believe that all are working towards the fulfilment of my good, they have to work towards the fulfilment of my good. I don't ask them. I don't compel them. I simply do it only within myself, and the whole vast world exists within me. Therefore, it is myself "pushed out." It's objectified. I don't have to change affairs; I only change it within myself; and then everyone, though I know him or not by name,—it doesn't really matter,—it's myself "pushed out."

I couldn't tell you the atoms of my body, but it is my body. I couldn't tell you if you took the handoff that it's my hand I am looking at, any more than I could tell you your name or anything about you; yet, you are myself "pushed out," as this body is the body I wear. And so, as the body obeys my mind, you—my "pushed-out" body—will obey my mind too. All I have to do is to concern myself with what I want in this world, and try to keep it within the frame of the Golden Rule;

doing unto others only that which I would want done unto me,—nothing more than that; hurting no one, doing not a thing to anyone other than that which I would want done unto me.

If you want all the lovely things done,—do only the lovely, and do it all in your own wonderful human imagination. Then you will realize this tremendous secret of imaging. It is the greatest of all secrets, to the solution of which everyone in the world should aspire, because Christ is the answer.

Christ is defined for us in the first chapter of First Corinthians as "the power of God and the wisdom of God" (First Corinthians 1:24). Here is the power of God and the wisdom of God; and I have found the power to be in myself.

"You mean, Christ is in me?" Are we not taught that in scripture? "Know ye not that Jesus Christ is in you? Do you not know that Jesus Christ is in you, unless of course you fail to meet the test?"

(Second Corinthians 13:5) Well then, test it. How would I test it?

A friend of mine, maybe, is unwell; or maybe he's unemployed, or maybe he is not earning enough to meet the obligations of life. All right, he is in me. As I think of him, he's in me. He need not be physically present for me to think of him; he's in me. I think of him; I conjure him. Well, can I change his entire picture in me? I assume that he is talking to me, and he's telling me that he has never had more, he has never felt better; and as I believe in what I am seeing in my own mind's eye,—I believe in him. That is Christ in me, and all things are possible to Christ. Well then, test it and see if it works. See if you do not see him in the not-distance future earning more, looking better; and everything in the world that you have done within you, he responds to. He need not praise you or thank you. You don't need his praise;

you don't need his thanks. You don't need confirmation from him, other than he does conform to what you have done in yourself concerning him.

You ask no one to thank you. Thank nothing. You are simply exercising the power of God within you. "And the power of God and the wisdom of God is Jesus Christ" (First Corinthians 1:24). And there is nothing in the world but God. It is all God in you "pushed out," and God is your own wonderful human imagination. He can't be closer. God is never so far off as even to be near, for nearness implies separation. He's not separated. God actually, literally became as I AM, that I may be as He is. He is not something on the outside. No matter how near He is, He can't even touch me. He actually became me, with all of my weaknesses, all of my limitations; and now I am trying to struggle within myself to find out who I AM,—and that's His name.

My name is in Him. What's your name? "Go and say I AM has sent you." "Is that you name?" "Yes, forever and forever it is my name." "What name? Jehovah?" "No." "The Lord?" "No, I AM." That's His name. That is His name forever and forever.

Well I cannot say, "I AM," and point elsewhere. I can't say, "I AM," and feel something is near me. It can't even be near. Something can be near to what I AM, but "I AM" can't be near. And that's the name of God forever and forever. So you are the Lord Jesus Christ.

Now a pattern is given to us in scripture by which you will know that you are; and I promise you, from my own personal experience, that you shall have it. It is a true story. The truest story ever told is the story of the Lord Jesus Christ. When He said, "I AM the Father," may I tell you, if he's a father, he has a son, hasn't he? Or at least he has a child; but I tell you, it's a son. He said,

"When you see me, you see the Father"; but if I look at you and I say, "Well then, you are the father, show me your son." He can't show me His son outside as His son, because He and I are one. He has to show me His son not of blood nor of the will of the flesh; it has to be born, not of blood nor of the will of the flesh nor of the will of man, but of God. And He tells me that He is God, and He tells me that He and I are one. Well then, it can't be born in any normal, natural way. He has to be born of God.

Well then, who is your son? He tells me in scripture that David calls Him, "Father."

"David calls you, 'Father'?"

"Yes." He said, "I inspired the prophets," and read the Prophets; and in the Prophets, David calls the Lord, "my Father."

"You mean, David, then, is my son?"

"Yes, he's my son."

"But I do not know him," you will say.

But I will tell you, from my own personal experience, you will know it because I know it; David called me, "my Father." David called me, "my Lord." David called me the Rock of his salvation. Everything that is said in scripture concerning what he said of the Lord, he said of me. And so, I stood, and here is David, and I knew it beyond all doubt that here is my son, and my son is David,—not a David,—the David—the only David—the David of biblical fame. And as he called me, "Father," memory returned.

So God actually became me, and then He unfolds Himself within me. Well, as He unfolds Himself within me, it's only the memory of God that He gave up in order to become me. He had to completely give up all that was God to become this little witness that is called a man called Neville. So when His memory returns and He became me, it is my memory returning. He actually gave me Himself as He gave you Himself; and the day will come as He unfolds Himself within you, your memory returns because it's God's memory returning. He completely empties Himself in order to become you.

This is the story of the Christian faith; the fulfilment of all the promises made in the Old Testament. The Old Testament is only a prophetic blueprint of the life of Jesus Christ. It's an adumbration, a foreshadowing in a not-altogether conclusive or immediately evident way; but as it unfolds within you, it's nothing more than God's memory returning. But having become you, it becomes your memory returning, and you awaken as God Himself. And there is nothing in the world like God.

Now you ask, what, all the horrors of the world, the pain, the suffering? Yes. It takes all the "furnaces" to prepare you to receive the gift that He gives, and the gift is Himself. God actually became you. He gave Himself to you, that you may be God. And God in you is your own wonderful human imagination, that's God.

Now tonight try it. I ask you to believe me. But whether you believe me or not, try it anyway. Take a friend of yours and bring him before your mind's eye, and then talk to him from the premise of your desire for him fulfilled—not going to be, but already fulfilled. And having done it, believe that all things are possible to the Lord Jesus Christ; and you just saw Jesus Christ in action, for you saw the creative power of God in action, and that's Jesus Christ. That is your own wonderful human imagination.

Now believe in the reality of what you've just done. Believe that this subjective appropriation of your objective hope for a friend is a fact. That is really praying. And all things are possible to God. Go within and appropriate it—just completely appropriate it, and see it unfold within your own vast marvellous world.

So this wonderful secret is the secret of the Lord Jesus Christ. If you turn on the outside and turn to another, you do not know the Lord Jesus Christ. You can make all kinds of images of Him. That's not the Lord Jesus Christ. If any man should ever come and say, "Look, there he is," or "Here he is," don't believe it. Why? Because when you actually meet Him, you are going to meet your Self. The Christ of faith comes to us as one unknown; yet one who in some ineffable mystery lets us experience who He is; and when we experience Jesus Christ, we experience Him in the first-person, singular, present-tense experience. You will never see Him coming from without. Let no one tell you you're going to meet Him coming from without. You will meet Him awakening Himself within you as you. That's the Lord Jesus Christ. That's the great sacrifice. He is crucified on Humanity.

Every human form is the cross that He wears; and in that form He awakens as the one in whom He awakens. He awakens as that Being, and that Being is the Lord Jesus Christ. And because He is the father of David, David called that Being, "Father"; then you know, "I AM He."

Oh, I can tell you from now to the ends of time, and I may not persuade you to believe it; but when it happens to you, you need no further persuasion, for you are confronted with the facts and there you stand in the presence of you own son, and the son is the Son of God.

"I will tell of the decree of the Lord," said David. "He said unto me, 'Thou art my son. Today I have begotten thee.'" (Psalm 2:7) These are the words of David in the Second Psalm. "I will tell of the decree of the Lord. He said unto me, 'Thou art my son.'" That son is going to call you, "Father"; and then, and only then, you will know you are God the Father. That is the mystery of the entire world. And so, what you accomplish in this world concerning finances is wonderful for you as an individual in the world of Caesar. What you do concerning the social world—all these things—it's marvellous; but you will only really fulfil your destiny as you fulfil scripture, for the purpose of life is to fulfil scripture.

"I have accomplished the work Thou gavest me to do." What work? All that the prophets spoke about me; and beginning with Moses and the prophets and the Psalms; he interpreted to them in all the scriptures the things concerning Himself. Then said he, "Scripture must be fulfilled in you," and the purpose of life is to fulfil scripture—the prophecy of God to man, for He gave man Himself, or promised to give man Himself. And He promised me a son. The son He promised was His Son; and in giving me His Son, He gave me Himself, for His Son calls me, "Father." And that is the whole mystery of life. There's nothing but God. One Being expanding Himself forever and forever and forever, each Himself. And even though he calls you, "Father," may I tell you, you will not lose your identity. You are individualized and you will tend towards ever greater and greater individualization. And yet, you are the Father of my son; and if you are the Father of my son, then you and I are one. It is a great mystery,—we are brothers,—for you do not lose your identity and I do not lose my identity. So you and I, behind these masks are eternal brothers—the Father of the One and only Begotten Son.

Well if you are the father of my son, and my own wife is the "father" of my son, then the relationship on earth of men, or friend to friend and wife to husband, is above this level, and we are eternal brothers, all forming the one Father.

So tonight, you take me seriously; and when you go home—or start it here,—you put into practice this greatest of all secrets; the secret of imaging. There is no greater secret in the world. Every child born of woman is alive because it was imagined. And imaging is God in action. That's the soul of man—imaging; and that is the power of God. And the power of God is Christ. And that is the wisdom of God, and the wisdom of God is Christ.

A child can imagine. Well, that's Christ. That is Christ crucified on that little tiny garment, and it suffers with everything that that little child imagines, or it enjoys with everything the little child imagines. It wears all the stripes and all the blows that man in his misuse of that power will do. He doesn't criticize him. He waits upon me as indifferently—and as quickly—when the will in me is evil as when it is good. That way, He bears all my stripes. He bears all of my misuse of His power, knowing that in the end, I will awaken and use it only lovingly.

When I completely awaken from the dream of life, I will use this creative power of God only lovingly. But in the meantime while I am trying to awaken to the use of this power, I misuse it. And may I tell you, you will confront this vision, and you will see what you did from the beginning, for you didn't begin it a few years ago in your mother's womb. You have been coming through the centuries.

One night, here I saw this monstrous creature covered in hair. It looked like a gorilla, and the hair was all dark brown from head to toe. It was a monster. And here, the most glorious, heavenly creature—a female; and this was a male monster. And it called out to this heavenly creature, "Mother, mother." Well, I knew this could not be—this radiant, heavenly creature; and so I struck him. And as I struck it, it gloated; it loved violence. And I pummelled it, and it gloated all the more. Well, it could speak in a guttural tone, calling this heavenly being, "Mother." And that annoyed me. Then suddenly from within me I knew. Why, this is my own creation. And so is this one. They are only the out picturing of my two different uses of the creative power that I AM.

Here (the monster) is the complete embodiment of every misused moment of my life. Every time I was violent, I created and fed this monster.

It whispered in my ear to be monstrous, to be violent, to be bad, to be evil, for it fed only on this thought. And here (the heavenly creature) was the embodiment of all my loving thoughts. Every kind, considerate, wonderful thought in my life fed this one.

As I saw this monstrous thing and realized that it was my own offspring,—it was the fruit of my misspent energy,—I pledged myself. There was no one to whom I could turn,—I pledged myself that if it took eternity I would redeem it. It did not come into being through any power other than my own misuse of my own power. It could not have been brought into being; and that thing could not live, and it could not help itself. I didn't condemn it.

At that moment, I felt compassion beyond the wildest dreams of anyone for this monstrous thing that I had created. And when I made myself that pledge that I would redeem it if it took me eternity, at that very moment, the whole thing got smaller and smaller and smaller; but it didn't waste—the energy that it embodied returned to me. I began to feel a power that, until that moment, I had never felt before. And this one began to grow. The beauty that she embodied and personified glowed as the energy came back from this one (the monster) to me; and the whole thing dissolved before my eyes.

So, "nothing is lost in all my holy mountain" I did not lose that energy that I misplaced,—it returned to me,—that was embodied in that monster. And throughout the centuries, it was it who whispered in my ear monstrous things to be done, because it could only feed on violence. It could only feed on evil.

Then I realized what it meant: that I ate of the Tree of the Knowledge of Good and Evil. And so it fed upon evil, and she fed upon the good. And then the evil that was only the energy misspent returned to me; and then the whole thing came back to me. And then I broke the spell, and I awoke in this world.

Well everyone is going to confront that gorilla on the threshold. Everyone has him, unseen by mortal eye, and he whispers into your ear to entertain the unlovely thoughts of the world. And your every reaction that is unlovely, it feeds upon it; and your every thought that is kind and wonderful and loving, she feeds upon it. And the day will come, you will be strong enough to confront this. And may I tell you, it will take you the twinkling of a second to dissolve it? You don't labor upon it. All it needs is the core of integrity within you. When you pledge yourself, and no one else,—you don't swear upon your mother, you don't swear upon a friend, you don't swear upon the Bible;

you pledge yourself to redeem it. At the moment you pledge yourself,—and within you, you know you mean it,—the whole thing dissolves. It's no time at all in dissolving. And then all the energy returns to you, and you are stronger than ever before to go forward now and eat of the Tree of the Knowledge of Good and Evil.

And if you forward and misuse it again, you start another form building; and one day you will dissolve it again. Eventually you will become completely awakened, and you will use your wonderful power only—not for good,—that tree will come to an end,—for Life itself. For eating of the Tree of the Knowledge of Good and Evil is this world. The day will come that you will eat of the Tree of Life that bears the fruit of truth and error. Error will embody itself here, and one day you will confront the error, and the error will dissolve before your mind's eye as truth begins to glow before you, because you are eating, then, of the Tree of Life as you formally ate of the Tree of the Knowledge of Good and Evil. And the combat of good and evil produces this monster, and the combat of truth and error produces an entirely different form of being, more glorious than that one of good and more horrible than this. The error will dissolve just as quickly when you confront error.

So if today your teaching is not true and you live by it, you are building something just as monstrous; but one day you will confront error and you will discover that you lived by a false concept of God—something on the outside of Self; that you formerly worshiped a little golden figure made of gold and silver. It had eyes, but could not see. It had ears, but could not hear. It had a mouth, but could not speak. It had feet, and it could not walk. It made no sound within its throat. And those who made it are just like it. And those who trusted it are just like it too.

So all the little icons in the world that people worship—these are the little things called "error"; and one day you will discover the true God. And when you discover the true God, you will find that He is all within your own wonderful being as your own wonderful human imagination. You'll walk in the consciousness of being God. You don't brag about it.

As Blake answered when they asked him, "What do you think of Jesus Christ?" Blake answered, "Jesus Christ is the only God"; but he hastened to add to it, "But so am I, and so are you."

So you don't tell anyone. You simply know that you are the Being spoken of in scripture as "God the Father." For all that is said of Him, you are going to experience; and you are going to experience it in the first-person, singular, and a present-tense experience. And then you will know.

Today is the eleventh year since it happened to me right here in this city, right across the way at the hotel with the star at the top of the roof, the Sir Francis Drake, on the 20th day of July 1959. It was then that I, at 4:00 in the morning, felt within my head the most intense vibration, and I thought, this is a brain hemorrhage, and this is it. I knew nothing of the human form, and I thought I cannot possible survive what I am feeling; so this must be what they call a massive brain hemorrhage. But instead of departing this world, I awoke to find myself within my own skull; and I knew that I was entombed completely within my own skull. I was fully awake, as I've never been awake before, and here I am sealed—the skull is sealed, and I AM in it. The skull is not a little thing like this (indicating the head). It's the size of a huge, big sepulcher, and I knew it to be my skull. I also know intuitively that I could get out by pushing the base of my skull. As I pushed it, a stone rolled away, and I saw the little opening, and I put my head through it and pushed; and I came out, inch by inch, just as a child is born from the mother's womb. But instead of being born from below of flesh and blood, I was "born from above" out of the skull—Golgotha, where Christ was buried. But it was not another coming out,—I am coming out. There was no other. I had no companion in that skull. I myself was there, and I came out. And when I looked back at the body out of which I came, it was ghastly pale, turning its head from side to side like one in recovery from a great ordeal. I stood up and looked at it, and then suddenly I heard this strange, strange wind—this unearthly wind that I had heard in the tomb within my head,—well now, it seemed to be divided and coming from the corner of the room.

As I looked over to see if it really came from that side, and I looked back three or four seconds later the body had been removed. There is no body; but in its place sat my three older brothers. My eldest sat where the head was, my second one sat where the right foot was, and the third one sat where the left foot was; and they heart this same unearthly wind. They couldn't see me. I not only saw them, I could read their thoughts as I could read my own. Their thoughts all were objective to me. Everything was objective. They couldn't have an emotion that wasn't objective. They couldn't have a thought that wasn't objective. And yet, I heard their voices.

And then my brother Lawrence got off the bed and started towards the same direction that I thought this wind originated—this peculiar wind. As he took one or two steps, he said, "Why, it's

Neville's baby. This is the cause of this peculiar, unearthly wind."

My brother Victor and my brother Cecil, they said, "How can Neville have a baby?"

He didn't argue the point. He lifted from the floor a little infant wrapped in swaddling clothes and brought it and placed it on the bed; and I took that infant up into my arms, and as I looked into its face and said, "How is my sweetheart," this little heavenly face broke into the most glorious smile; and then the whole scene dissolved.

There was the resurrection from the dead, followed by the "birth from above." So we are "born from above," as told us in the Book of Peter. "We are born anew through the resurrection of Jesus Christ from the dead." (First Peter 1:3) There is only one Being resurrected, the Being who descended into man; and that is Jesus Christ. He descended into man, the power of God and the wisdom of God, and united with man; and when they became one and fulfilled the destiny of that Being, only He now wakes as you. And so, you awake as the Lord Jesus Christ, without loss of identity.

So eleven years ago on the 20th day of July, back in 1959 here in this city, that drama took place within me. So it is my birthday today in a spiritual sense. The little body that now stands before you, that came in the year 1905. It will depart and turn into dust; but that which awoke within me is the Immortal Self that cannot die. And those who have not had the experience, that Immortal Self is still there, and it cannot die. You will be restored to life in a world just like this to continue the drama until that experience that I've just told you takes place within you.

Nothing dies. The little rose that bloomed once, blooms forever. It turns to ash as the body will turn to ash, but you—the Immortal You, who is all imagination—cannot die. But it will awaken one day in the same manner that it awoke within me. It was buried in Golgotha, which means "the skull." He is buried on Calvary, which is the skull. It is in the skull of man that God is buried; and there God-in-man will awake.

So here this night you put it to the test as you are challenged in scripture to test Him. And you test, not another, you test your own wonderful human imagination, for that is the Lord Jesus Christ.

The truest story ever told is the story of Jesus Christ. Let the world rise in opposition and say there is no Lord. As Blake brought out so beautifully in his poem "Jerusalem":

"... Babel mocks; saying there is no God or Son of God;

That Thou, O Human Imagination, O Divine Body of the Lord Jesus Christ art all A delusion; but I know Thee, O Lord, when Thou arisest upon My weary eyes, even in this dungeon and this iron mill...

For Thou also sufferest with me, although I behold Thee not.

… And the Divine Voice answers,

… Fear not. Lo, I AM with you always,

Only believe in me, that I have the power to raise from death Thy Brother who sleepeth in Albion."

You can't get away from your own imagination. You can't get away from it because that's your own being. That is the reality. But it suffers with you. He is the Lord Jesus Christ within you. Now test Him tonight. Test Him for the good. Do you want a better job when they say they are letting people out? Forget what the papers say. Forget what anything says. "All things are possible to the Lord Jesus Christ." (Matthew 19:26)

If you don't have enough money, forget what the paper says, you assume that you have it. "All things are possible to God." He sets no limits whatsoever on the power of believing. Can you believe it? We'll try to believe it. Try to believe, first of all, in God. Well God is your own imagination. Well believe in Him; that whatever you can imagine is possible.

Can you imagine that you have now the kind of a job that you want? The income that would come from it? The fun in the doing of the work? Well then walk as though it were true; and to the best of your ability believe that it's true. And that assumption though denied by your senses,—though the world would say it is false; if you persist in it, it will harden into fact. This is the law of your own wonderful imaging. Believe it, and it will become a reality.

OTHER BOOKS YOU MAY LIKE

- 1984 by George Orwell, ISBN: 9789380914947
- 12 Years a Slave by Solomon Northup, ISBN: 9789390492374
- 51 Most Powerful Prayers by Ryan, ISBN: 9789354990847
- A Christmas Carol by Charles Dickens, ISBN: 9788193545874
- A Cloud by Day, a Fire by Night by AW Tozer, ISBN: 9789354990854
- A Passage to India by E.M. Forster, ISBN: 9789354990205
- A Room of One's Own by Virginia Woolf, ISBN: 9789354990281
- A Streetcar Named Desire by Tennessee Williams, ISBN: 9788194748601
- A Wrinkle in Time by Madeleine L'Engle, ISBN: 9789354991066
- Abraham Lincoln by Lord Charnwood, ISBN: 9789380914251
- Absolute Surrender by Andrew Murray, ISBN: 9789389716269
- Animal Farm by George Orwell, ISBN: 9789380914701
- Anthem by Ayn Rand, ISBN: 9789389157079
- As a Man Thinketh by James Allen, ISBN: 9788180320262
- As I Lay Dying by William Faulkner, ISBN: 9789390492381
- Awakened Imagination by Neville Goddard, ISBN: 9789389157086
- Be What You Wish by Neville Goddard, ISBN: 9789387669550
- Chanakya Neeti by Chanakya, ISBN: 9789389716276
- Civilization and Its Discontents by Sigmund Freud, ISBN: 9789387669499
- Delighting in God by AW Tozer, ISBN: 9788194748632
- Demian by Hermann Hesse, ISBN: 9789387669567
- Experiencing the Holy Spirit by Andrew Murray, ISBN: 9788194764809
- Feeling is the Secret by Neville Goddard, ISBN: 9789389157109
- George Orwell Combo : Animal Farm & 1984, ISBN: 9789390492459
- Gravity by George Gamow, ISBN: 9789388118484
- Guerrilla Warfare by Ernesto Che Guevara, ISBN: 9789354990366

Develop your reading habit | **Gift books to your friends**

OTHER BOOKS YOU MAY LIKE

- How to be filled with the Holy Spirit by AW Tozer, ISBN: 9789389157116
- How to Develop Self Confidence by Dale Carnegie, ISBN: 9789387669000
- In His Steps by Charles M. Sheldon, ISBN: 9789390492794
- Life of Christ by Fulton J. Sheen, ISBN: 9789389716306
- Lost Horizon by James Hilton, ISBN: 9789389716313
- Man: The Dwelling Place of God by AW Tozer, ISBN: 9789354990656
- Maneaters of Kumaon by Jim Corbett, ISBN: 9789354990731
- Mansarover 1 (Hindi) by Premchand, ISBN: 9789380914978
- Mansarover 2 (Hindi) by Premchand, ISBN: 9789380914985
- Meditation and Its Methods by Swami Vivekananda, ISBN: 9789389716320
- One, None and a Hundred Thousand by Luigi Pirandello, ISBN: 9789389716337
- Paths to Power by AW Tozer, ISBN: Forthcoming
- Scientific Healing Affirmations by P. Yogananda, ISBN: 9789389716344
- Selected Stories of Rabindranath Tagore by Tagore, ISBN: 9789380914770
- Siddhartha by Hermann Hesse, ISBN: 9789380914145
- Student's Encyclopedia of G. K. by GP Editors, ISBN: 9789380914190
- Tales from Shakespeare by Charles Lamb & Mary Lamb, ISBN: 9789380914367
- The Alchemy of Happiness by Al-Ghazzali, ISBN: 9789387669505
- The Book of Enoch by Enoch, ISBN: 9789390492480
- The Dynamic Laws of Prosperity by Catherine Ponder, ISBN: 9789388118156
- The Game of Life and How to Play It by Florence Shinn, ISBN: 9789387669390
- The Imitation of Christ by Thomas À Kempis, ISBN: 9789388118057
- The Knowledge of the Holy by AW Tozer, ISBN: 9789389157130
- The Law by Neville Goddard, ISBN: 9789390492886
- The Light of Asia by Sir Edwin Arnold, ISBN: 9789380914923
- The Magic of Believing by Claudie Bristol, ISBN: 9789388118149

Develop your reading habit | **Gift books to your friends**

OTHER BOOKS YOU MAY LIKE

- The Magic of Faith by Joseph Murphy, ISBN: 9789388118743
- The Miracles of Your Mind by Joseph Murphy, ISBN: 9788180320743
- The Mysterious Affair at Styles by Agatha Christie, ISBN: 9789390492510
- The Origin of Species by Charles Darwin, ISBN: 9788180320453
- The Plague by Albert Camus, ISBN: 9788194764892
- The Power of Awareness by Neville Goddard, ISBN: 9789387669406
- The Power of Positive Thinking by Norman Vincent Peale, ISBN: 9789388118569
- The Problem of Increasing Human Energy by Nikola Tesla, ISBN: 9789354990953
- The Prophet by Kahlil Gibran, ISBN: 9789380914022
- The Psychopathology of Everyday Life by Sigmund Freud, ISBN: 9789388118071
- The Pursuit of God by AW Tozer, ISBN: 9789389157147
- The Railway Children by E Nesbit, ISBN: 9789354990960
- The Red Badge of Courage by Stephen Crane, ISBN: 9789354990977
- The Sound and the Fury by William Faulkner, ISBN: 9789390492572
- The Stranger by Albert Camus, ISBN: 9789390492589
- The Sun Also Rises by Ernest Hemingway, ISBN: 9789354990984
- The Yoga Sutras of Patanjali by Patanjali, ISBN: 9789389716351
- Their Eyes Were Watching God by Zora Neale Hurston, ISBN: 9788194764885
- Think and Grow Rich by Napoleon Hill, ISBN: 9788180320255
- Thought Vibration by William Walker Atkinson, ISBN: 9789389157154
- To the Lighthouse by Virginia Woolf, ISBN: 9789390492190
- Who were the Shudras by Dr B.R. Ambedkar, ISBN: 9789354991028
- World's Best Short Stories: Volume 1 by Various Authors, ISBN: 9789390492275
- Wuthering Heights by Emily Brontë, ISBN: 9788193545898
- Your Faith is Your Fortune by Neville Goddard, ISBN: 9789389157161
- Zen in the Art of Archery by Eugen Herrigel, ISBN: 9789354991059

Develop your reading habit | **Gift books to your friends**

www.ingramcontent.com/pod-product-compliance
Ingram Content Group UK Ltd.
Pitfield, Milton Keynes, MK11 3LW, UK
UKHW040228300826
14791UKWH00001B/38

9 789354 991271